OUR SCHOOL SIGNS

British Sign Language
(BSL)
Vocabulary

by
Cath Smith

D1470766

CO-SIGN COMMUNICATIONS

FROM CO-SIGN COMMUNICATIONS (inc DeafBooks.co.uk)

LET'S SIGN DICTIONARY EVERYDAY BSL: 2nd Edition Revised & Enlarged

LET'S SIGN POCKET DICTIONARY: BSL Concise Beginner's Guide

BSL 100 EVERYDAY SIGNS: Beginner's Handbook

BSL QUESTION SIGNS

BSL FAMILY SIGNS

BSL EMERGENCY CONTACT SIGNS

LET'S SIGN FOR WORK: BSL Guide for Service Providers **2nd Edition**

SIGN LANGUAGE LINK: A Pocket Dictionary of Signs

LET'S SIGN FAMILY TOPICS: BSL for Children and their Carers

Signs of Health: A Pocket Medical Guide

BSL Describing People

LET'S SIGN & DOWN SYNDROME: Signs for Children with Special Needs

LET'S SIGN SCIENCE: BSL Vocabulary for KS 1, 2, & 3 (Dictionary)

A CHILD'S BOOK OF SIGNED PRAYERS (Kindle)

EARLY YEARS

LET'S SIGN EARLY YEARS: BSL Child and Carer Guide **2nd Edition**

LET'S SIGN BSL EARLY YEARS & BABY SIGNS: Poster/Mats A3 Set of 2

LET'S SIGN BSL: EARLY YEARS CURRICULUM TUTOR BOOK

LET'S SIGN BSL: EARLY YEARS CURRICULUM STUDENT BOOK

BSL SIGN & SPELL ABC Alphabet Book

BSL Halloween Signs: Colouring & Activity book

BSL CHRISTMAS SIGNS for Family Learning

BSL BABY SIGN LINK BOOK (with QR code links to videos of signs)

GOLDILOCKS & THE 3 BEARS BSL Sign & Word Activity Book

BSL CLOTHES SIGNS

BSL VEHICLE SIGNS

BSL Mini Topics for Tots

BSL Food & Drink for Tots

BSL OPPOSITES

FLASHCARDS

LET'S SIGN BSL: Early Years & Baby Signs FLASHCARDS

LET'S SIGN BSL: FEELINGS & EMOTIONS FLASHCARDS

LET'S SIGN BSL : House & Home FLASHCARDS

BSL CHRISTMAS SIGNS Flashcard Format (Kindle)

LET'S SIGN BSL THANK YOU CARDS - LET'S SIGN BSL REWARD STICKERS

(Most of the above publications are also now available in Kindle format)

GRAPHICS PACKS - On annual licences for creating your own materials
see www.Widgit.com

LET'S SIGN BSL: Full Adult Dictionary Set Graphics Pack

LET'S SIGN BSL: Baby & Early Years Graphics Pack

LET'S SIGN SCIENCE: BSL (KS 1, 2, & 3) Graphics Pack

First published 2017, updated 2022

ISBN-13: 9781905913527

ISBN-10: 1905913524

Published by Co-Sign Communications
(inc.DeafBooks)
Stockton-on-Tees TS18 5HH

Tel: 01642 580505
email: info@deafbooks.co.uk - info@letssign.co.uk
www.DeafBooks.co.uk - www.LetsSign.co.uk

The Let's sign BSL graphics and Widgit Symbols packs are available on licence for creating bespoke materials from www.widgit.com

ACKNOWLEDGEMENTS

Grateful thanks and appreciation go to;

Suzanne Williams and Laura Philips of the Deaf and Hearing Impairment Team (DAHIT), Leeds City Council for their help with suggestions of words/signs for inclusion.

Sandra Teasdale, Sara Mclanaghan, and David Hugill of MeSign BSL British Sign Language Specialists for their help with the technology and social media terms.

Printed by Amazon Print-on-Demand

CONTENTS

THE SIGN VOCABULARY

INTRODUCTION

If there are pupils or classmates in your school who use signs in their everyday learning and communication then this book is for you. It contains a basic introduction to the signs needed for the day to day interactions and experiences in school settings (primary and secondary) - school activities and instructions plus vocabulary to enable peer conversations that will be useful to classmates and school staff alike.

The sign vocabulary contained is from British Sign Language (BSL). This is the the language of the Deaf community in Britain and also forms the basis of other signing systems used in education in the field of Special Educational Needs (SEN).

This book focuses on the use of signs in education - with deaf children and adults and for the even greater numbers of adults and children with Special Educational Needs who use BSL signs in their learning and communication.

The most commonly used signs and regional variations are included but please check for local usage through face-to-face contact and classes taught by qualified Deaf tutors.

The Let's Sign BSL series of publications and comprehensive dictionaries are recommended resources for supporting learners - see details on the back page.

BRITISH SIGN LANGUAGE (BSL)
It Makes Sense

Sign languages are used all over the world, but they are not all the same language. They are visual gestural languages with their own syntax and grammar. They share similar features and structures but each has its own vocabulary and variations - even other English speaking countries (such as America) have their own separate sign language.

See page 109.

SIGN SUPPORTED ENGLISH (SSE)

Sign Supported English (SSE) is a form of sign language that encourages the use of spoken language with signs for key-words used simultaneously.

It is widely used in education to great effect with children who have learning disability and additional speech, language and communication needs associated with, for example, Down Syndrome, autism and cerebral palsy.

SSE is a common element of BSL used in deaf education. It is used by some deaf adults and as a contact language in interactions between the Deaf community and the hearing world.

The signs contained in this book can be ordered in the visual gestural grammatical structures of BSL - or used alongside spoken English as Sign Supported English depending on the situation and the individual needs of each user.

Acquiring language requires meaningful and accessible exchanges with those around us if language and learning are to be achieved.

Most deaf children are born to hearing parents (approx. 90%) who may have no prior knowledge of sign language, just as the families of children with special needs are also likely to be new to signing.

Children and families who need sign language are themselves likely to be in the ongoing process of learning it.

ADVANTAGES OF SIGN LANGUAGE

There are many advantages to learning BSL and fingerspelling that can prove an asset to most children's development. It can aid communication with pre-verbal infants and the visual and kinaesthetic elements add extra dimensions to language and communication that some children are extremely responsive to, and all children can potentially benefit from.

There are developments to include BSL as a school language option and also exciting development work with BSL key word support for children for whom English is not a first language.

This groundswell of interest in and respect for BSL is greatly welcome but it is also ironic that BSL was for generations banned in deaf education and continues to be omitted from educational use for many deaf children - due at least in part to lingering beliefs that signing hinders spoken language development (in spite of evidence to the contrary).

It was not until the 1980's that BSL started to re-emerge in deaf education and this relatively recent development by no means applies to all deaf children.

There is a general misconception that all deaf children use sign language and attend special schools but studies show:

• There are at least 41,377 deaf children in England.

• Only 10% of deaf children use sign language in some form, either on its own or alongside another language.

• 78% of school aged deaf children are in mainstream settings where there is no specialist provision.

Consortium for Research into Deaf Education (CRIDE) report 2015. (See www.batod.org.uk).

The number of youngsters who are not deaf but have other special educational needs and have the benefit of signs to support learning and communication is far greater, although the exact figures are not known.

The opportunity for all children to have effortless communication with their educators and peer group should be a given - but without special steps to encourage the wider acceptance and use of sign language in education, it will remain a lottery, based on individual school and educational policy, making it even more important that all pupils and staff gain a basic working knowledge of sign language.

THE IMPORTANCE OF THE FACE

The hands may be signing but it's the face that tells the story. The face is the focus of our communication generally and for sign languages in particular.

> One of the most important features of BSL is termed NON-MANUAL FEATURES (top left example opposite). This refers to the expressive use of face and body that compacts information into the manual signs made by the hands.
>
> The good news for learners is that reading faces is a universal phenomenon and that the conscious and unconscious messages we give out in this way are used and understood the world over.

Learners typically focus on the hands and movements of the signs, often temporarily forgetting their natural ability to convey meaning non verbally, and yet it is the face that is the starting point and the focus for communicating in BSL. Attention is focused on the eyes, lip-patterns and expressions whilst the signing is taken in by peripheral vision.

If part of the face is obscured or turned away it becomes more difficult to read the meaning. Eye contact and face-reading are also important for the development of rapport and empathy.

In addition to relevant information such as concern, fear, anger and so on, non-manual features in BSL can give very specific grammatical information too. For example, puffed cheeks are used to emphasise intensity - an important part of the process of compacting extra detail into signs.

Think visually and use your imagination!

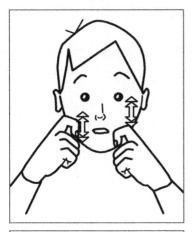

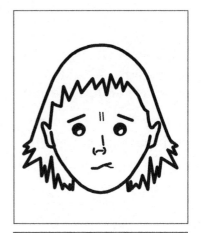

IT'S NOT WHAT YOU SIGN
IT'S THE WAY THAT YOU SIGN IT!

The pictures on this page and the page opposite illustrate how your face and non-manual features can change what you mean even though the sign is the same.

Signs are more densely packed than words. You can question, or agree, or disagree.

don't have to

have to

now?

now

WHAT OUR FACE SAYS

Nodding the head in affirmation, shaking in negation, raising the eyebrows in question form or a stern face for a command can all take place simultaneously with sign production.

See how the face changes the meaning in these signs to make 'who?' become 'someone'. Can you see the difference?

have to!

who?

now!

someone

BSL BASIC HANDSHAPES

These are frequently used handshapes in BSL and terms used in this resource to describe them.

The fingers are identified (from the thumb) as *index finger, middle finger, ring finger* and *little finger.*

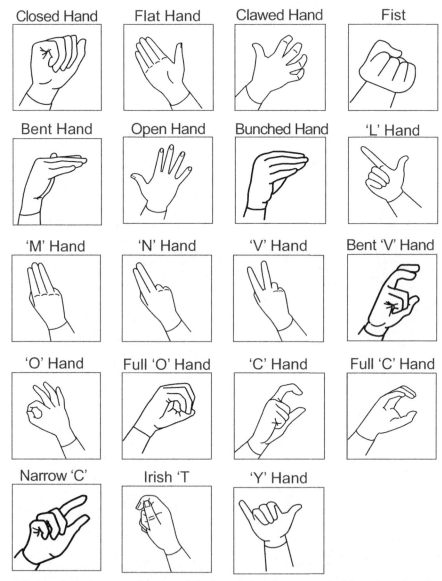

Closed Hand	Flat Hand	Clawed Hand	Fist
Bent Hand	Open Hand	Bunched Hand	'L' Hand
'M' Hand	'N' Hand	'V' Hand	Bent 'V' Hand
'O' Hand	Full 'O' Hand	'C' Hand	Full 'C' Hand
Narrow 'C'	Irish 'T	'Y' Hand	

All signs are drawn with the right hand dominant and abbreviated as R.
Left handed signers will use the left hand as dominant.
Left hand is abbreviated as L.

THE ROLE OF FINGERSPELLING IN BSL

- Fingerspelling is an important and integral part of BSL but relies on the understanding of the English words and should be used with caution.

- Fingerspelling represents each letter of the alphabet on the hands and can be used to spell out whole words, abbreviated forms or initials.

- It can be used to spell out names for people and places.

- It is often used for commonly occurring small words, that become recognised as signs eg. **'SON'**, **'DAY'**, **'SO'**, **'FOR'**, **'HOW'** - even where a sign may exist.

- It is best learned in word patterns and rhythms and needs practise.

- Lip-pattern should reflect the whole word and not individual letters.

- It uses abbreviated forms eg. **'SFF'** - STAFF, **'JAN'** - JANUARY and repeated initials eg. **'KK'** - KITCHEN, **'FF'** - FATHER, **'MM'** - MOTHER, **'WW'** - WEDNESDAY, **'TT'** - TOILET and so on.

- Months of the year are similarly fingerspelt abbreviations or the shorter words are spelt in full, eg. **'MAY'**, **'JUNE'**.

- It is an important and integrated feature of BSL and gives a direct link to English.

BRITISH
FINGERSPELLING
ALPHABET
LEFT-HANDED VERSION

A	B
C	D
E	F
G	H
I	J
K	L
M	N
O	P
Q	R
S	T
U	V
W	X
Y	Z

BRITISH FINGERSPELLING ALPHABET RIGHT-HANDED VERSION

		A	B

C	D	E	F

G	H	I	J

K	L	M	N

O	P	Q	R

S	T	U	V

W	X	Y	Z

FINGERSPELLING: DAYS OF THE WEEK

Days of the week in BSL are usually initialised as shown below - either by a single fingerspelt initial letter as shown in the top 6 examples (MONDAY to SATURDAY from top left), or by a repeated initial as in the sign drawing set, or by abbreviations such as 'MON' 'TU' or 'TUES' 'WED' 'TH' or 'THURS' 'FRI' 'SAT' as in the bottom 6 examples.

MONDAY TUESDAY WEDNESDAY THURSDAY FRIDAY SATURDAY

MONDAY TUESDAY WEDNESDAY THURSDAY

FRIDAY or FRIDAY SATURDAY or SATURDAY

SUNDAY

SUNDAY is signed with the flat hands tapping together twice, although SATURDAY and SUNDAY do have alternative signs in some regions.

WEEKEND

MONDAY TUESDAY WEDNESDAY THURSDAY FRIDAY SATURDAY

DAYS OF THE WEEK: SCOTLAND

A separate system for days of the week is used in many parts of Scotland. The index finger and thumb tap together twice for MONDAY, the middle finger and thumb for TUESDAY, the ring finger and thumb for WEDNESDAY and little finger and thumb for THURSDAY.

FRIDAY is signed with R. palm left 'V' hand moving right to left across the chin. SATURDAY is a repeated downward opening movement of a closed hand held under the chin, and SUNDAY is palm left R. flat hand bending back to contact upper chest twice.

SATURDAY and SUNDAY also have alternative versions in some regions.

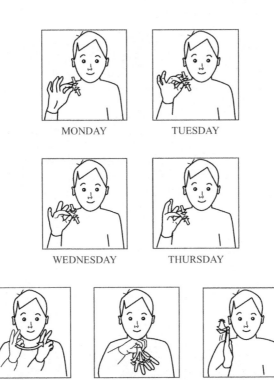

MONDAY　　　　TUESDAY

WEDNESDAY　　　THURSDAY

FRIDAY　　SATURDAY　　SUNDAY

MONTHS OF THE YEAR

Months are usually fingerspelt either in full or contracted forms as in the examples below. The months follow left to right going down the pages.

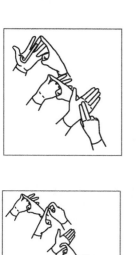 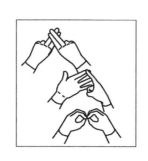 

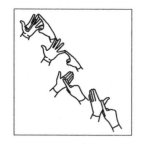 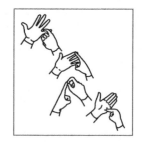 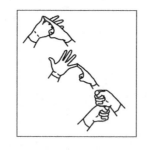

  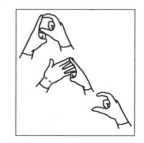

FINGERSPELLING GAME

See how many words of 3 or more letters you can make from the word COMMUNICATION. You can try this on your own or work in teams with one 'recorder' per team.

Without voice, take turns to fingerspell your word to the recorder to write down and see who can find the most words after an agreed time.

Mouth the full word when you spell it - don't mouth individual letters. Keep practicing individual words and you will feel a rhythm and pattern starting to emerge.

Here are a few to start you off......teachers too!.......

Down page L. to R. - cat, cot, cut, tan, tin, ton, mint, moon, onion, union, nation, notion.

NUMBERS: Quick Reference Guide

Numbers are notorious for their regional variations. It is not possible to show them all in this simple guide, but the two most commonly used and understood systems are illustrated.

Learners need to be aware of their own regional versions and variations used in other areas.

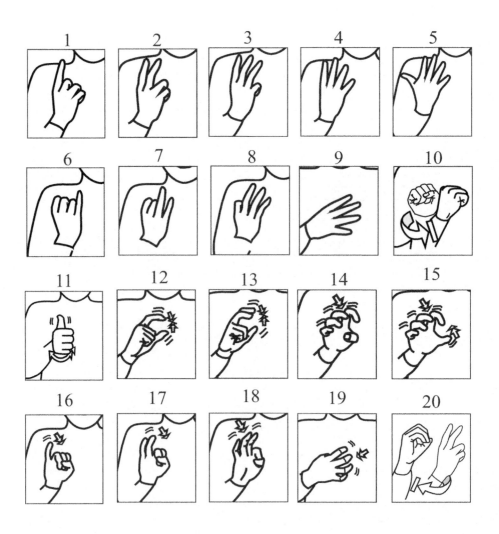

20 is illustrated - 30, 40, 50, 60 etc. start with the relevant number handshape for 3, 4, 5, (6 and so on from either system) followed by zero, up to 90.

Other numbers over 20, sign the first digit then the second ie 2 then 1 as in 21 shown on the right and so on with the relevant numbers from your regional system.

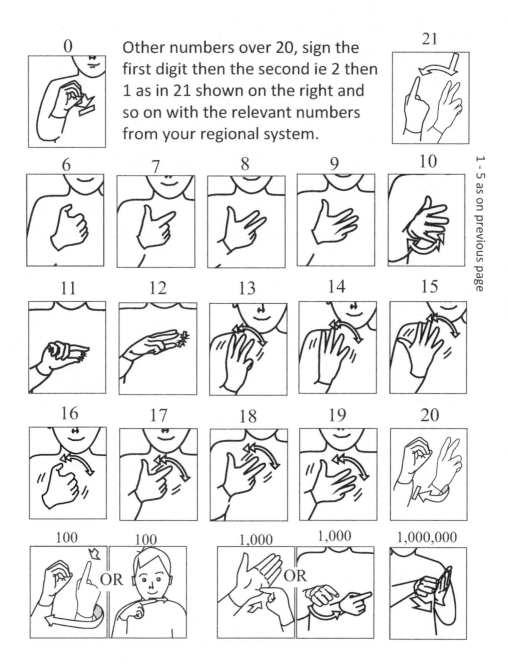

SIGNS IN CONTEXT
Directional Verbs

Like words in spoken language, signs can vary a great deal in context when in use. Some verbs change direction to correspond with the subject and object in the context they are used, which makes good sense visually and shows again how extra detail can be compacted into signs.

Below are three simple examples of verbs **HELP, GIVE** and **EMAIL**. The top row shows *I'll help, I give, I'll email* moving away from the signer and the bottom row shows *help me, give me* moving back towards the signer and *email me* which twists round to flick backwards towards the signer.

I'LL HELP   I GIVE   I'LL EMAIL

HELP ME   GIVE ME   EMAIL ME

SIGNS IN CONTEXT
Inflections

Other signs can be inflected to make visual sense in context. These examples show the 'V' hand used to represent the direction and movement of eye-gaze in context.

The sign **LOOK** moves from the eyes and can point and move in different ways to suit the context, such as sweeping up and down in *look up and down* or in a sideways wavy movement in *look around* and twisting sharply back to the signer in *look at me.*

ASK moves forward for the general sign and *I'll ask,* but twists and moves back to the signer for *ask me* or sweeps round to indicate a group of people in *ask everyone.*

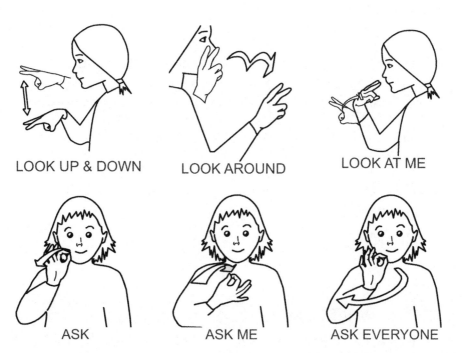

LOOK UP & DOWN   LOOK AROUND   LOOK AT ME

ASK   ASK ME   ASK EVERYONE

GETTING ACQUAINTED

HELLO, HI

HELLO, FINE, OK?

WELCOME, RECEPTION

HOW ARE YOU?

FINE, FIT, WELL

ARE YOU WELL?

HEARING,

HEARING PERSON

DEAF, DEAF PERSON

PROFOUNDLY DEAF

I/ME

YOU

LIKE

DON'T LIKE

FAVOURITE

BEST

MY, MINE, MY OWN

YOUR, YOURS,

YOUR OWN

OUR

NAME

WHAT?

WHO?

SOMEONE

WHICH?

HOW OLD?

WHY? WHAT FOR?

BECAUSE, REASON

WHEN?

HOW MANY?

WHAT TIME?

WHERE?

LIVE, ADDRESS, (TOILET)

SIGN, SIGN LANGUAGE

FINGERSPELL, SPELL

SLOW, SLOWLY, A LONG TIME

AGAIN, REPEAT,

FREQUENTLY, OFTEN

PLEASE, THANK YOU

GOOD MORNING

GOOD AFTERNOON

GOOD EVENING, NIGHT

GOODBYE, BYE, (HELLO)

BYE-BYE

MOBILE PHONE

TEXT MESSAGE, SMS

WIFI

FACEBOOK

EMAIL

SOCIAL NETWORK

SKYPE

FACETIME

INTERNET

WEBSITE

GOOGLE

CONTACT, CONNECT, JOIN

GETTING ACQUAINTED

HELLO, HI

Flat hand with thumb tucked in makes short movement out from near side of head.

HELLO, FINE, OK?

Closed hands with thumbs up twist sharply over from palm down to palms facing. With raised brows means OK?

WELCOME

Fingers of palm up bent hands bend backwards several times in beckoning movements.
Also means RECEPTION.

HOW ARE YOU? FINE, FIT, WELL

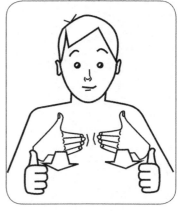

Bent hands touch chest then move forward closing with thumbs up. With raised brows also means ARE YOU WELL?

GETTING ACQUAINTED

HEARING, HEARING PERSON

Index finger moves from ear to mouth. May finish with repeated tap on the chin.

DEAF, DEAF PERSON

'N' hand contacts ear. Cheeks may be puffed for emphasis for example in PROFOUNDLY DEAF.

I, ME

Tip of extended index finger contacts the chest.

YOU

Index finger points with short movement towards the person referred to or with sideways sweep for plural.

GETTING ACQUAINTED

LIKE

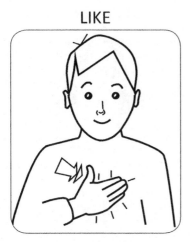

Flat hand taps chest twice with pleased expression.

DON'T LIKE

Open hand on chest twists forwards/up and away from the body as the head shakes with negative expression.

FAVOURITE

Palm down closed hands, with thumbs out.
R. thumb contacts chin, as both hands make firm movement down.

BEST

Tip of R. extended thumb brushes forward sharply against the top of L. extended thumb.

GETTING ACQUAINTED

MINE, MY, MY OWN

Closed hand moves back to contact upper chest. Also means BELONGS TO ME.

YOUR, YOURS (singular)

Palm forward closed hand is directed towards the person referred to. Sweeps sideways for plural. Also means YOUR OWN, BELONGS TO YOU.

OUR

Palm forward closed hand sweeps round to end palm back on chest. Also means BELONGS TO US.

NAME

Tips of 'N' hand touch side of forehead, then move and twist forward.

GETTING ACQUAINTED

WHAT?

Palm forward index finger makes small side-to-side shaking movements, eyebrows raised or furrowed in question form.

WHO?

Upright index finger makes small horizontal circles, eyebrows raised or furrowed. With neutral expression also means SOMEONE.

WHICH?

'Y' hand moves from side-to-side or between the objects or persons referred to, eyebrows raised or furrowed.

HOW OLD?

Fingers of palm back hand wiggle in front of the nose, eyebrows raised or furrowed.

GETTING ACQUAINTED

WHY? WHAT FOR?

Edge of R. index taps
left upper chest twice,
eyebrows raised or
furrowed. With neutral
expression, also means
BECAUSE, REASON.

WHEN?

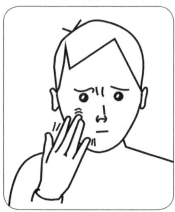

Fingers wiggle at side of
the face, eyebrows raised
or furrowed.

HOW MANY?

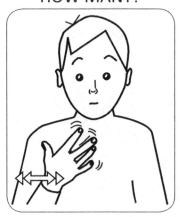

Fingers of palm back
hand wiggle as hand
moves from side-to-side.
Can be signed with both
hands moving apart.

WHAT TIME?

R. index finger pointing
up near shoulder waggles
from side-to-side (WHAT)
then taps back of L. wrist
(TIME).

GETTING ACQUAINTED

WHERE?

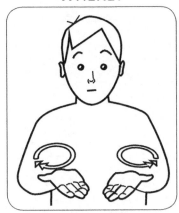

Palm up hands move in small outward circles, or hands may shake in and out towards each other, eyebrows raised or furrowed.

LIVE, ADDRESS

Tip of middle finger rubs up and down on side of chest. Also a regional sign for TOILET.

SIGN, SIGN LANGUAGE

Palm facing hands make forward circular movements round each other.

FINGERSPELL, SPELL

Fingers and thumbs wiggle against each other as hands move to the right. Refers to two-handed fingerspelling.

GETTING ACQUAINTED

SLOW, SLOWLY

R. index finger (or flat hand) moves slowly along and up left forearm from the wrist. Also means A LONG TIME.

AGAIN, REPEAT

Palm left 'V' hand shakes forward/down from the wrist twice. Also means FREQUENTLY, OFTEN.

PLEASE, THANK YOU

Tips of flat hand touch mouth, then hand swings forward/down to finish palm up.

GOOD MORNING

Closed hand with thumb up (GOOD) then tips of R. bent hand contact left then right side of upper chest (MORNING).

GETTING ACQUAINTED

GOOD AFTERNOON

Closed hand with thumb up (GOOD) then fingers of 'N' hand touch chin and twist from wrist to point forwards (AFTERNOON).

GOOD EVENING, NIGHT

Closed hand with thumb up (GOOD) then palm back flat hands at sides of face swing in/down to finish crossed (EVENING, NIGHT).

GOODBYE, BYE

Hand held up waves from side to side. This sign is also used for HELLO.

GOODBYE, BYE-BYE

Palm forward flat hand bends repeatedly from palm knuckle.

GETTING ACQUAINTED

MOBILE PHONE

Hand with fingers tightly curled is held near the ear.

TEXT MESSAGE, SMS

Palm up Irish 'T' hand; thumb flexes repeatedly as hand moves in small circles.

WIFI

Fingers of palm down R. open hand flutter forward and back from L. upright index finger.

FACEBOOK

Palm forward hands are held at sides of the face and tap twice on the cheeks or make opening/closing movements.

EMAIL

Index fingers flick off thumbs towards each other twice. Can be one hand only in direction to suit context (see page 22).

SOCIAL NETWORK

Palm down R. open hand circles round upright L. index then index fingers and thumbs interlock and move round in a circle.

SKYPE

Backs of clawed hands held back to back tap together twice.

FACETIME

R. hand makes up and down signing movements towards palm back clawed hand held forward.

GETTING ACQUAINTED

INTERNET

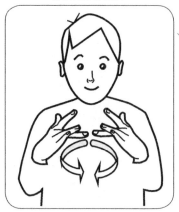

Tips of middle fingers touch then hands move out and round in circular shape and then contact again.

WEBSITE

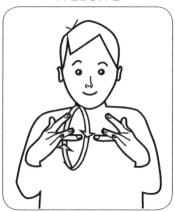

Tips of middle fingers touch; L. hand remains stationary as R. hand moves in forward circle then contacts again.

GOOGLE

Full 'O' hands make small inwards twisting movements in front of the eyes.

CONTACT, CONNECT

Hands move towards each other and fingers of 'O' hands interlock. Also means JOIN.

GETTING ACQUAINTED

LINK THE SIGN TO THE WORD

MINE

DEAF

WHAT TIME?

BEST

BYE

GOOD AFTERNOON

THANK YOU

LIVE

PEOPLE

MAN, MALE

WOMAN, LADY, FEMALE

BOY

GIRL

HEAD, PRINCIPAL, AUTHORITY, BOSS, EMPLOYER

TEACHER, TUTOR

STAFF

STUDENT, PERSON

FRIEND

PARENT/S

MOTHER, FATHER

STRANGER

INTERPRETER

COMMUNICATION SUPPORT WORKER (CSW)

HELP

SOCIAL WORKER

DOCTOR

NURSE

AUDIOLOGIST

CLEANER

POLICE

SPEECH THERAPIST

TEACHING ASSISTANT

TEACHER OF THE DEAF, TUTOR

VISITOR

PEOPLE

MAN, MALE

Fingers and thumb stroke down chin as thumb closes onto fingers. May repeat.

WOMAN, LADY, FEMALE

Palm forward index finger brushes forward twice across cheek.

BOY

Extended R. index finger brushes across chin to the left. May repeat.

GIRL

Palm forward index finger brushes forward twice across cheek in small movements.

PEOPLE

HEAD, PRINCIPAL

Index fingers pointing
forward/up flick sharply
up/back from wrists.
May be one hand only.
Also means AUTHORITY,
BOSS, EMPLOYER.

TEACHER, TUTOR

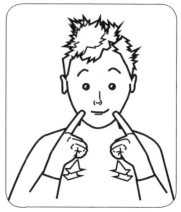

Index fingers near sides of
the mouth move forward
and apart in two short
movements.

STAFF

Fingers of palm back R.
'V' hand are drawn across
the left upper arm.

STAFF

Fingerspell 'S' then
repeated 'FF'.

PEOPLE

STUDENT, PERSON

Palm forward narrow 'C'
hand moves down.

FRIEND

Hands clasp together and
shake forward/down
several times.

PARENT/S

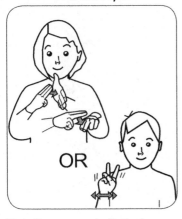

Tap fingerspelt 'M', then
'F' (MOTHER, FATHER)
OR palm forward 'V'
hand in front of shoulder
shakes side-to-side.

STRANGER

Palm back open hand
moves forward from in
front of the face and
closes with index held up.

PEOPLE

INTERPRETER

'V' hands twist alternately backwards and forwards from the wrists.

COMMUNICATION SUPPORT WORKER

'C' hands move alternately forward/back (COMMUNICATION); R. fist on L. palm moves forward (SUPPORT, HELP) then edge. of R. hand taps on L. at right angles (WORK) - or fingerspell 'CSW'.

SOCIAL WORKER

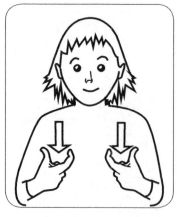

Fingertips of 'C' hands move down sides of chest. May repeat. 'SW' or 'S worker' also sometimes used.

DOCTOR

Tips of R. hand middle finger (or index, or both) and thumb grasp left wrist. May tap twice.

PEOPLE

NURSE

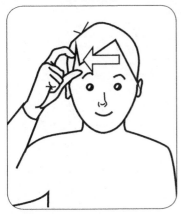

Tips of 'C' hand are drawn across the forehead or thumb tip makes a cross on left upper arm.

AUDIOLOGIST

Clawed hands tap sides of head over ears twice, or make twisting movements.

CLEANER

Palm forward closed hands move alternately in repeated inward circular rubbing movements.

POLICE

Fingers of R. 'V' hand flex slightly as hand is drawn across back of L. wrist.

SPEECH THERAPIST

Palm back bent 'V' hand makes small circles in front of the mouth then closed hands with thumbs up, move forward together, one behind the other (SUPPORT).

TEACHING ASSISTANT

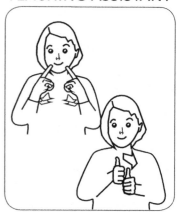

Index fingers at sides of mouth make two short forward movements (TEACHER) then closed hands, thumbs up move forward one behind the other (SUPPORT).

TEACHER OF THE DEAF

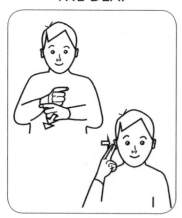

Indexes extended held R. on L. at an angle as hands make two short movements forwards (also TUTOR) then fingers of 'N' hand touch ear.

VISITOR

Palm back 'V' hands, slightly overlapping, move in short forward arc together.

PEOPLE

LINK THE SIGN TO THE WORD

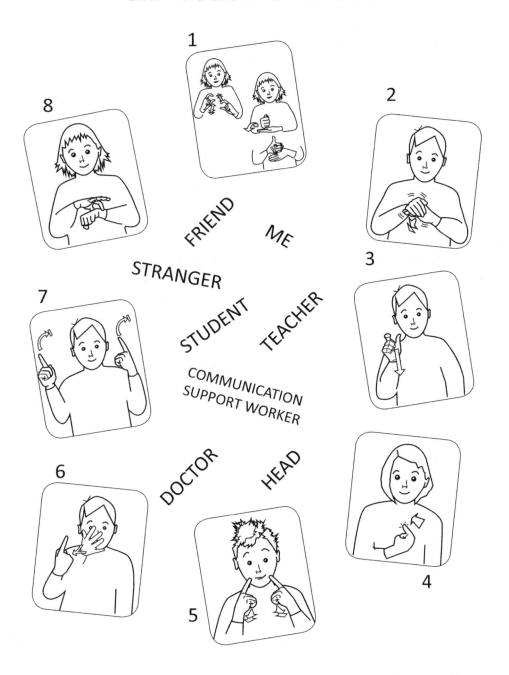

FRIEND

ME

STRANGER

STUDENT

TEACHER

COMMUNICATION SUPPORT WORKER

DOCTOR

HEAD

SCHOOL THINGS

COAT	PAPER
SHOE/S	iPAD, TABLET
REGISTER, ENROL,	GLASSES
NAME DOWN	HEARING AID
PACKED LUNCH,	COCHLEAR IMPLANT
EAT, FOOD	UNIFORM
BAG	RULES
PENCIL, PEN	MUST, HAVE TO
PENCIL SHARPENER	SMART, TIDY
RUBBER, ERASER	SAME
BOOK	DIFFERENT
DICTIONARY	EASY, SIMPLE
RULER	HARD, DIFFICULT

SCHOOL THINGS

COAT

Closed hands move down
and round from shoulders
in action of putting coat
on.

SHOE/S

R. full 'C' hand palm
down (or palm up) slots
onto L. hand. Repeat L.
onto R. for plural.

REGISTER

'N' hand touches side of forehead (NAME) and then bent 'V'
hand contacts L. palm (ENROL,
NAME DOWN) and repeats
downwards like a list of names.

PACKED LUNCH

Bunched hand makes two
short movements to the
mouth (EAT, FOOD) then
closed hand makes two short
downward movements (BAG).

SCHOOL THINGS

BAG

Palm back closed hand makes short repeated downward movements.

PENCIL, PEN

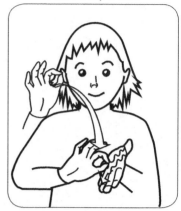

'O' hand moves down from behind the ear to wiggle across L. palm. Second part only for PEN.

PENCIL SHARPENER

R. Irish 'T' hand makes repeated twisting movements at the side of L. fist.

RUBBER, ERASER

R. Irish 'T' hand makes repeated rubbing movements on L. palm.

SCHOOL THINGS

BOOK

Flat hands start palm to palm, then twist open and apart.

DICTIONARY

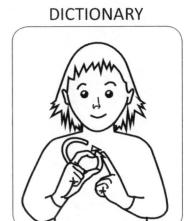

R. 'C' hand forms a fingerspelt 'D' and makes repeated circles against L. index, or same motion on L. palm.

RULER

Narrow 'C' hands move apart in outline shape, palm forward or palm down.

PAPER

Tap knuckles of both closed hands together twice or index fingers outline a sheet of paper.

SCHOOL THINGS

iPAD, TABLET

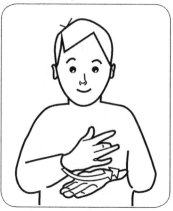

Tip of R. middle finger swipes repeatedly across palm of L. hand.

GLASSES

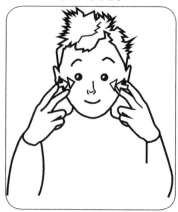

Palm back 'V' hands tap against upper cheeks twice near the eyes. One hand can be used.

HEARING AID

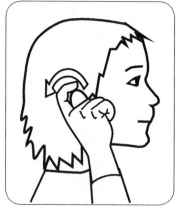

Bent index finger makes backward twisting movement over the ear.

COCHLEAR IMPLANT

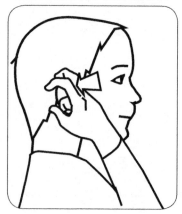

Tips of bent 'V' hand contact side of head above/behind the ear.

SCHOOL THINGS

UNIFORM

Tips of extended thumbs move simultaneously down the chest. Also one version of SMART.

RULES

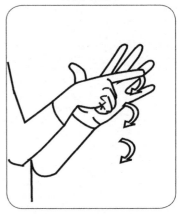

Edge of R. index finger moves down from L. palm in small hops.

MUST, HAVE TO

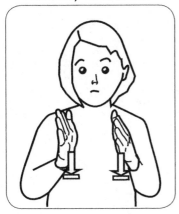

Flat hands held apart make short firm downward movement with stress.

SMART, TIDY

Fingers of 'N' hand tap twice against the side of the nose.

SCHOOL THINGS

SAME

Index fingers pointing forward contact each other. May tap twice or make single contact.

DIFFERENT

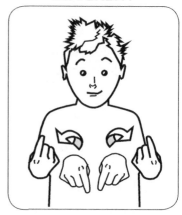

Index fingers pointing forward contact each other then twist over and apart.

EASY, SIMPLE

Index finger prods into the cheek twice. The cheeks may be puffed.

HARD, DIFFICULT

Tip of R. thumb prods into L. palm twice, eyebrows furrowed.

SCHOOL THINGS

LINK THE SIGN TO THE WORD

1

8

2

SHOES   BAG

REGISTER

3

7

PENCIL   iPAD

BOOK

PACKED LUNCH   UNIFORM

6

4

5

IN SCHOOL & CLASSROOM

TERMS, SEASONS

AUTUMN

SPRING, GROW

SUMMER

SUMMER, HOT

WINTER, COLD

BREAK, REST, HOLIDAY, AT EASE

HOLIDAY, VACATION

SCHOOL

RECEPTION

CORRIDOR, HALL, PASSAGEWAY

DINING ROOM, REFECTORY

LIBRARY

CLASS, CLASSROOM

TUTOR GROUP

STUDY PERIOD

KEY GROUP

TOILET

BOYS' TOILET

GIRLS' TOILET

SHOWERS,

STAIRS

LOCKER

CUPBOARD

FLIP CHART

WHITE BOARD

DOOR, OPEN DOOR, CLOSE DOOR

WINDOW

CHAIR, SIT DOWN

DESK

SHELF

TABLE

OFFICE

NOTICE BOARD, POSTER

LAB

COMPUTER ROOM

ASSEMBLY

LESSON

BELL, ALARM

FIRE ESCAPE

EMERGENCY EXIT

PLAYGROUND

TERMS, SEASONS

Palm back hands are held about 6 inches apart, one in front of the other as they move forward in small jumps. Single movement for singular.

AUTUMN

Fingers of R. hand wiggle moving down at side of L. hand held upright (TREE). Can also be signed with both hands moving down, fingers wiggling.

SPRING

Fingers of R. bunched hand spring open as it pushes up through fingers of L. slightly cupped hand Also means GROW.

SUMMER

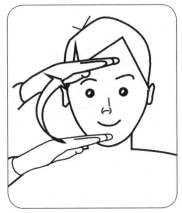

R. flat hand contacts chin then moves up in small arc to contact forehead. With negative expression also one version of STRANGER.

SUMMER, HOT

Flat hand (or index finger)
strokes left to right across
forehead finishing with a
small forward/downward
flick.

WINTER, COLD

Closed hands and elbows
pull into body in shivering
action, shoulders hunched,
cheeks puffed.

BREAK, REST, HOLIDAY

Thumb tips of open hands
(or just one hand) contact
the chest, head tilted,
lips pushed forward. Also
means AT EASE.

HOLIDAY, VACATION

Flat hands facing sides
of head, swing slightly
forward/apart twisting
to palm forward.

IN SCHOOL & CLASSROOM

SCHOOL

Palm back flat hand
makes side-to-side
shaking movements in
front of mouth.

SCHOOL

Index edge of flat hand
taps left upper chest
twice. This version also
means PARK.

SCHOOL

Palm forward 'N' hand in
front of the mouth shakes
from side-to-side in
downward wavy
movement.

RECEPTION

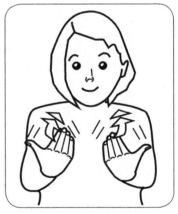

Flat hands bend back-
wards in short repeated
movements.

CORRIDOR, HALL

'N' hands move forward from sides of head. Flat hands can be used. Also means PASSAGEWAY.

DINING ROOM, REFECTORY

'N' hands move up and down alternately to the mouth (DINE, MEAL) then indexes pointing down move in square outline shape (ROOM).

LIBRARY

Palm together hands open (BOOK) then edge forward R. flat hand makes several short forward movements as it moves to the right.

CLASS, CLASSROOM

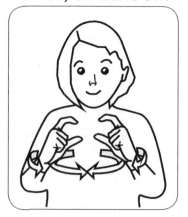

'C' hands face each other then twist apart and round to finish touching with palms facing back.

IN SCHOOL & CLASSROOM

TUTOR GROUP

Indexes extended held R. on L. at an angle as hands make two short movements down (TUTOR) then full 'C' hands swivel round to touch together at fingertips (also one version of CLASS).

STUDY PERIOD

Palm back flat hands move slightly side-to-side (STUDY, READ) then palm facing hands make short movement forward/down (PERIOD, UNIT).

KEY GROUP

R. hand taps down twice onto tip of L. index (also means IMPORTANT) then open hands with curved fingers come together (GROUP).

TOILET

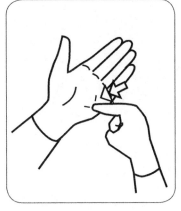

Repeated fingerspelt 'T'. There are a number of other regional variations for TOILET.

IN SCHOOL & CLASSROOM

BOYS' TOILET

R. index brushes to the right across chin (BOY) then repeat fingerspelt 'T' or other variation for TOILET.

GIRLS' TOILET

R. index brushes forward twice across cheek (GIRL) then repeat fingerspelt 'T' or other variation for TOILET.

SHOWERS

Full 'O hand above head, bends down as fingers spring open several times.

STAIRS

Fingers of bent 'V' hand wiggle in diagonal upwards movement.

IN SCHOOL & CLASSROOM

LOCKER

Closed hand moves backwards in action of opening a locker door.

CUPBOARD

Closed hands move backwards in action of opening cupboard doors.

FLIP CHART

'O hand moves up and over top of upright L. flat hand.

WHITE BOARD

'O' hand brushes down twice near collar (WHITE) then index fingers trace outline shape of board.
(NB COLOURS VARY REGIONALLY)

DOOR

R. hand pivots forwards and back from the wrist onto back of palm back L. hand. Forward for OPEN DOOR, backwards for CLOSE DOOR.

WINDOW

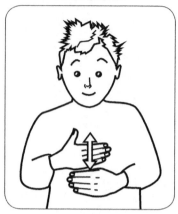

R. palm back flat hand moves up and down on top of L.

CHAIR, SIT DOWN

Palm down fists make short firm movement down.

DESK

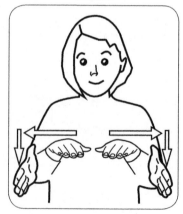

Palm down flat hands move apart then twist to palm facing and move down.

IN SCHOOL & CLASSROOM

SHELF

Palm down flat hands at shoulder height move apart.

TABLE

Palm down flat hands in front of the body move apart.

OFFICE

Palm forward 'O' hand moves round in small circles.

NOTICE BOARD

Extended thumbs press forward at head height, and then move down and repeat lower down. Also means POSTER.

IN SCHOOL & CLASSROOM

LAB

Fingerspell 'L A B'.

COMPUTER ROOM

Fingers of palm down hands wiggle (COMPUTER, TYPE) then indexes pointing down move in outline shape of room.

ASSEMBLY

Open hands held apart and facing, twist over/down towards each other like a gathering of people. The sign SUNDAY (PRAY) page 16 is also used.

LESSON

Palm forward 'L' hand moves down in side-to-side wavy movement.

IN SCHOOL & CLASSROOM

BELL, ALARM

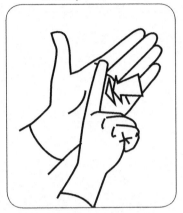

Side of extended R. index finger bangs twice against the L. palm.

FIRE ESCAPE

Palm facing hands move up, fingers wiggling (FIRE), then R. extended index moves sharply forward under palm down L. hand (ESCAPE).

EMERGENCY EXIT

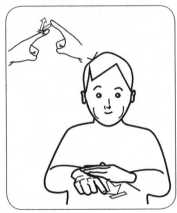

R. index bangs sharply on L. index and bounces up again (EMERGENCY, QUICK, SUDDEN, URGENT) followed by sign for ESCAPE.

PLAYGROUND

Palm up open hands move in small outward circles (PLAY) then palm down open hands move apart (GROUND).

IN SCHOOL & CLASSROOM

LINK THE SIGN TO THE WORD

STAIRS

CLASS

HALL

CHAIR   ALARM

DINING ROOM

TOILET   PLAYGROUND

SUBJECTS

TIMETABLE,

GRAPH

SUBJECTS,

TITLE, TOPIC

LANGUAGE

ENGLISH

GERMAN

FRENCH

SPANISH

BUSINESS

ICT

SCIENCE,

CHEMISTRY

MATHS, NUMBER,

DATE

MATHS,

CALCULATE,

SUMS

MUSIC

P E, GYM

SPORTS

ART, DESIGN, DRAW

RELIGIOUS STUDIES,

PRAY

HISTORY,

LONG TIME AGO

GEOGRAPHY

DEAF STUDIES

SOCIOLOGY,

SOCIAL WORK

PHILOSOPHY,

THEORY

POLITICS

DESIGN & TECHNOLOGY

ENGLISH LANGUAGE

ENGLISH LITERATURE

HEALTH & SOCIAL CARE

SEX EDUCATION

SRE, SEXUALITY

RELATIONSHIPS EDUCATION

TECHNOLOGY,

ENGINEER/ING

COOKERY,

FOOD TECHNOLOGY

MEDIA STUDIES

DRAMA, THEATRE

EXAM

SUBJECTS

TIMETABLE

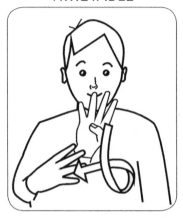

Palm forward open hand with thumb tucked in moves down, twists over to palm back and moves right. Also means GRAPH.

SUBJECTS

Fingers of palm facing 'V' hands flex several times (also means TITLE, TOPIC) or fingerspelt abbreviation 'S J'.

LANGUAGE

Palm forward 'L' hands move apart. Hands may start palm back and twist forward and apart.

LANGUAGE

Fingers of R. flat hand brush to the right across L. palm, may repeat.

SUBJECTS

ENGLISH

R. index finger rubs
back and forth along the
length of L. index finger.

GERMAN

Side of hand with index
finger extended taps
front of forehead twice.

FRENCH

Index finger closes onto
thumb as hand moves
out from side of the face.

SPANISH

Palm back Irish 'T' hand
on left upper chest twists
over to palm forward.

SUBJECTS

BUSINESS

Little finger edge of palm
up flat hand taps into
side of body twice. Also a
regional sign for TOILET.

ICT

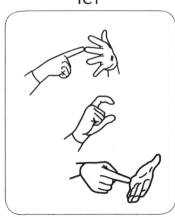

Fingerspell 'ICT'.

SCIENCE

Full 'C' hands make
alternate tipping
movements in front of
the body. Also means
CHEMISTRY.

MATHS, NUMBER

Knuckles of closed hand
tap chin twice. Also
means DATE and with raised
eyebrows, HOW MANY?

SUBJECTS

MATHS

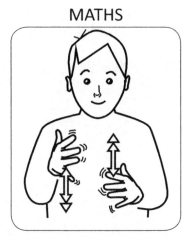

Palm back hands move up and down alternately as fingers wiggle. Also means CALCULATE, SUMS.

MUSIC

Palm forward index fingers (or 'O' hands) swing in and out towards each other several times.

PE, GYM

Fingertips of bent hands move up and down on shoulders several times.

SPORTS

Palm forward R. flat hand twists sharply palm down in forward movement brushing against side of palm down L. hand.

SUBJECTS

ART

Palm back 'N' hand moves down in side-to-side wiggling movement. Also means DESIGN, DRAW.

RELIGIOUS STUDIES

Flat hands held palms together make short repeated movements forward/down. Also means PRAY.

HISTORY

Palm back flat hands circle backwards round each other over right shoulder. Also means LONG TIME AGO.

GEOGRAPHY

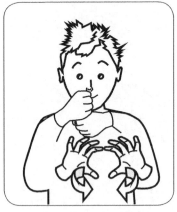

Fingerspell 'G' followed by curved hands moving apart and down in spherical shape (EARTH, WORLD).

SUBJECTS

DEAF STUDIES

'N' hand contacts ear.
(DEAF) then palm back
flat hands move upwards
near the face (STUDY).

SOCIOLOGY, SOCIAL WORK

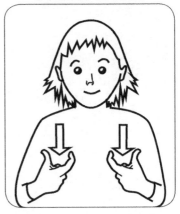

Fingertips of 'C' hands
move down sides of
chest. May repeat.

PHILOSOPHY

Fingers of palm down open
hand wiggle as hand moves
repeatedly backwards and
forwards from forehead.
Also means THEORY.

POLITICS

Palm down 'O' hands
move alternately up and
down.

SUBJECTS

DESIGN & TECHNOLOGY

R. 'V' hand taps L. palm, twists and repeats several times (DESIGN, PLAN) then palm back clawed hands twist in to intermesh (TECHNOLOGY).

ENGLISH LANGUAGE

R. index rubs back and forth along L. index (ENGLISH) then palm forward 'L' hands move apart (LANGUAGE).

ENGLISH LITERATURE

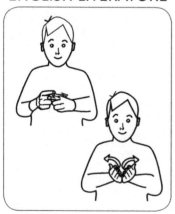

R. index rubs back and forth along L. index (ENGLISH) then palm to palm flat hands twist apart (BOOK).

HEALTH & SOCIAL CARE

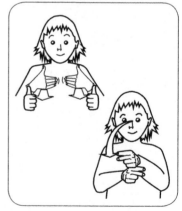

Tips of bent hands on chest move forward closing, thumbs up (HEALTH) then 'V' hands one on top of the other move down (CARE).

SUBJECTS

SEX EDUCATION

Index and little fingers extended from closed hands tap together twice (SEX) then bunched hands nod forward from sides of head (TEACH, EDUCATE).

SRE

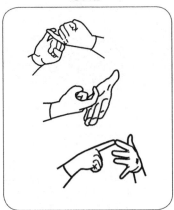

Fingerspell 'S R E'. Abbreviated form of **SEXUALITY RELATIONSHIPS EDUCATION**

TECHNOLOGY

Palm back clawed hands swing down/in towards each other so that fingers intermesh. Also means ENGINEER/ING.

COOKERY, FOOD TECHNOLOGY

Irish 'T' hand makes whisking movements in crook of left arm.

SUBJECTS

MEDIA STUDIES

R. hand with index, middle finger and thumb extended moves down to land firmly on back of palm down L. hand.

DRAMA, THEATRE

R. hand swings from side-to-side brushing tip of bent middle finger across the back of L. hand.

EXAM

Index edge of R. 'N' hand pointing forward rubs forward and back along L. palm several times.

EXAM

Closed hands held together at an angle twist round to change places.

SUBJECTS

LINK THE SIGN TO THE WORD

ART DRAMA

ENGLISH

COOKERY

MUSIC NUMBER

HISTORY SPORTS

CONDUCT & BEHAVIOUR

BEHAVE, BEHAVIOUR,
CALM, PATIENCE
POLITE,
GOOD, ALL RIGHT
BAD, AWFUL
TRUTH, HONEST,
PROMISE
LIE, LIAR, FIB
ARGUE, QUARREL
SWEAR, CURSE
CLASH, FIGHT,
CONFLICT
CHEEK, CHEEKY,
RUDE,
BAD MANNERS
IMPOLITE
INTERRUPT,
BUTT IN
CHEAT, SLY,
FOUL PLAY
BULLY, PROVOKE,
BULLYING ME
TROUBLE, NUISANCE,
PEST, NAUGHTY
LAZY, IDLE
STUPID, SILLY,
DAFT, FOOLISH

TEASE, JOKE, FOOL BETTER,
IMPROVE/MENT,
PROGRESS
ATTITUDE
RESPONSIBLE, DUTY
PRIVATE, CONFIDENTIAL
OBEDIENCE, RESPECT
HELP, ASSIST, SUPPORT
LOOK AFTER, CARE FOR,
CARETAKER, JANITOR
TRY, ATTEMPT
EFFORT, HARD WORK, BUSY
CONFIDENCE, CONFIDENT
CLEVER, BRIGHT
CONCENTRATE
CAREFUL, TAKE CARE
QUIET, QUIETLY
LATE, CLOCK
NOISE, NOISY, LOUD
IGNORE, TAKE NO NOTICE,
NEGLECT
SORRY, APOLOGISE,
MISTAKE
FORGIVE
SORRY, MISTAKE,
ACCIDENT/AL,
EXCUSE ME

CONDUCT & BEHAVIOUR

BEHAVE, BEHAVIOUR

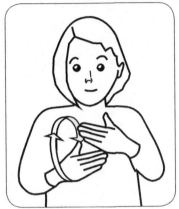

Flat hands brush
alternately down the
body in backward down-
ward circular movements.
Also means CALM,
PATIENCE.

POLITE

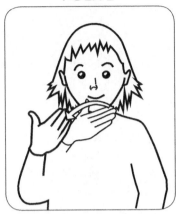

Fingers of R. flat hand
move slowly left to right
across the chin.

GOOD, ALL RIGHT

Closed hand (or both
hands) with thumb up
makes short movement
forward. Both hands can
be used for emphasis.

BAD, AWFUL

Extended little finger
makes short movement
forward. Both hands can
be used for emphasis.

CONDUCT & BEHAVIOUR

TRUTH, HONEST

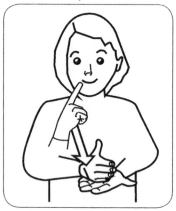

R. index finger moves
from mouth changing to
flat hand banging edge
down on L. palm. Also
means PROMISE.

LIE, LIAR, FIB

R. index finger is drawn
sharply to the right,
brushing across the chin.

ARGUE, QUARREL

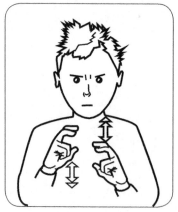

Bent 'V' hands facing
each other move up and
down alternately in
aggressive manner.

SWEAR, CURSE

Extended little finger
moves sharply forward
from mouth brows
furrowed.

CONDUCT & BEHAVIOUR

CLASH, FIGHT

Closed hands, little fingers extended, clash firmly together and may bang together several times. Also means CONFLICT.

CHEEK, CHEEKY, RUDE

Bent index and thumb grasp cheek and make small shaking movements.

RUDE, BAD MANNERS

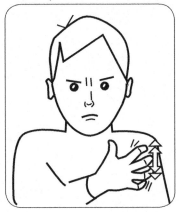

Tips of R. clawed hand rub up and down left upper arm. Also means IMPOLITE.

INTERRUPT, BUTT IN

R. flat hand moves sharply forward through fingers of L. hand (eg *can I butt in*?) or back to signer (eg *don't interrupt me*).

CONDUCT & BEHAVIOUR

CHEAT

Tip of thumb is drawn down the cheek, eyes narrowed and head tilted forward. Also means SLY, FOUL PLAY.

BULLY, PROVOKE

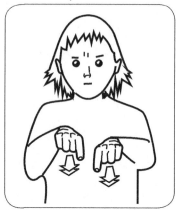

Index fingers make jabbing movements forwards towards the person being referred to. Can twist to point and move back to signer for BULLYING ME.

TROUBLE

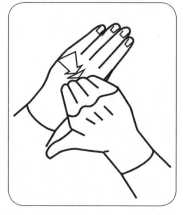

Tips of R. bent hand tap back of L. twice. Also means NUISANCE, PEST and one version of NAUGHTY.

LAZY, IDLE

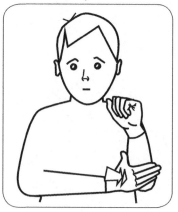

R. bent hand taps left elbow twice, tip of tongue between teeth.

CONDUCT & BEHAVIOUR

STUPID, SILLY

Palm up R. fist taps upwards to hit underside of L. palm (or side of head) twice. Also means DAFT, FOOLISH.

TEASE, JOKE, FOOL

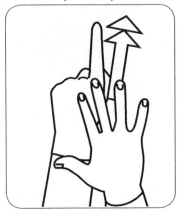

Palm down hands; R. open hand brushes forwards twice along L. index finger. Can twist to point and move back to signer for TEASING ME.

BETTER, IMPROVEMENT

Tip of R. extended thumb makes two small forward brushing movements against top of L. thumb.

IMPROVE/MENT

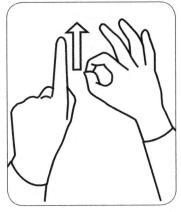

R. 'O' hand moves upwards on upright L. index finger. Also means PROGRESS.

CONDUCT & BEHAVIOUR

ATTITUDE

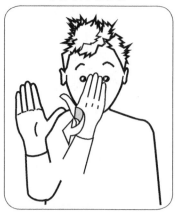

Flat hand palm back in
front of face twists to
palm forward.

RESPONSIBLE, DUTY

Bent hands (or 'N' hands)
one on top of the other,
move down onto
shoulder.

PRIVATE,
CONFIDENTIAL

Index edge of flat hand
taps twice against the
lips.

OBEDIENCE, RESPECT

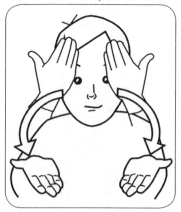

Flat hands touch
forehead, then swing
forward and down to
finish palm up, head
bowed.

CONDUCT & BEHAVIOUR

HELP, ASSIST

Hands move forward, closed hand with thumb up on L. palm (eg *I'll help*) or back to signer (eg *help me*) Also means SUPPORT.

LOOK AFTER

R. 'V' hand on top of L. at an angle; hands move down from near eye. Also means CARE FOR and CARETAKER, JANITOR.

TRY, ATTEMPT

R. extended index finger brushes forward twice against L. or with single movement.

EFFORT, HARD WORK

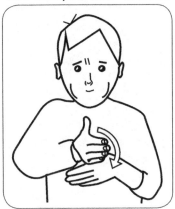

R. flat hand swivels forward/down over back of L. Cheeks may be puffed for emphasis. Also means BUSY.

CONDUCT & BEHAVIOUR

CONFIDENCE, CONFIDENT

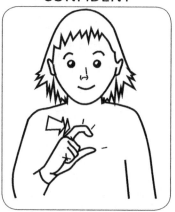

'C' hand taps the chest twice. May move down the chest for LOSE CONFIDENCE up the chest for GAIN CONFIDENCE .

CLEVER, BRIGHT

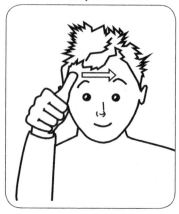

Tip of extended thumb moves sharply right to left across the forehead.

CONCENTRATE

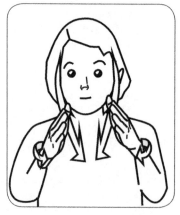

Flat hands at sides of head move forward/ down and twist in from wrists.

CAREFUL, TAKE CARE

'C' hands move forward/ down from near eyes. Index fingers may start straight and flex as they move.

CONDUCT & BEHAVIOUR

QUIET, QUIETLY

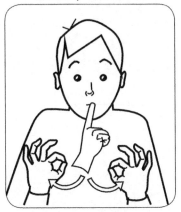

Index finger to lips then
'O' hands swing slowly
down and apart.

LATE

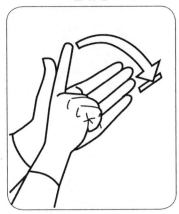

R. index finger twists
sharply forward/down
across L. palm. Index
waggles forward/down
twice for CLOCK.

NOISE, NOISY, LOUD

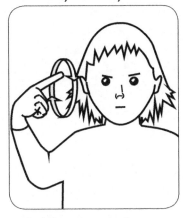

Index finger pointing
to ear makes repeated
forward circles.

IGNORE,
TAKE NO NOTICE

Head turns away as
index finger on ear twists
sharply down and away.
Also means NEGLECT.

CONDUCT & BEHAVIOUR

SORRY, APOLOGISE

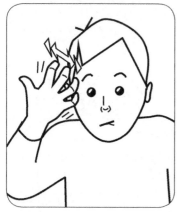

Closed hand rubs in circles on the chest with appropriate expression. Also another version for MISTAKE.

APOLOGISE, FORGIVE

Tips of R. flat hand touch mouth then rub in small circles on L. palm.

SORRY, MISTAKE

Clawed hand shakes side-to-side at side of head (or side of chin). Also means ACCIDENT/AL and another version for APOLOGISE.

EXCUSE ME

Tips of R. hand contact lips , then rub across   L. palm. Fingerspelt 'E X' is also used.

CONDUCT & BEHAVIOUR

LINK THE SIGN TO THE WORD

CONFIDENT

SORRY

LATE

RUDE

TRY

EXCUSE ME

INTERRUPT

LOOK AFTER

INSTRUCTIONS

READY

SIT DOWN

START, BEGIN

DON'T, NOT, NO

TALK, CHATTER

LAUGH

SING

INSIDE, INDOORS

OUTSIDE, OUTDOORS, HOME

CUT & PASTE

DRAW

PAINT

PICTURE, DIAGRAM,

CHART, LETTER

KEYWORD

WRITE, WRITE DOWN,

PEN, TAKE NOTES

DISCUSS, CONVERSE

PAIRS

INDIVIDUAL, ALONE,

INDEPENDENT

SIT IN A CIRCLE

SHOW ME

CHOOSE, PICK,

SELECT

ROLE-PLAY,

PERFORM/ANCE

TIME TO GO

COPY

DOWNLOAD

NOT SURE, UNSURE

DON'T UNDERSTAND,

OVER MY HEAD

THINK, SENSIBLE

REMEMBER, MEMORISE

FORGET, FORGOTTEN

CONCENTRATE, FOCUS

ASK

ANSWER, REPLY,

FEEDBACK

RIGHT, CORRECT

WRONG, WHAT'S WRONG?

CHECK, TEST

LOOK

LISTEN

LEARN

READ

SAY, TELL

INFORMATION, STORY

EXPLAIN, STORY

NEXT, TURN

SHARE

YES

NO

STOP, FINISH, END

STAND UP, GET UP

PUT AWAY

TIDY UP

LINE UP, QUEUE

QUICK, QUICKLY

PLAY TIME

DINNER/LUNCH TIME

WAIT, NOT YET

WAIT, STOP, HOLD ON

WASH HANDS

HOME TIME

TODAY, NOW, RIGHT NOW

AFTER, LATER

TOMORROW

YESTERDAY

PRACTICE, TRAIN

IMPORTANT, CRUCIAL, TOP

WELL DONE, CONGRATULATIONS

BRILLIANT, FANTASTIC

INSTRUCTIONS

READY

Thumb tips of open
hands tap upper chest
twice.

SIT DOWN

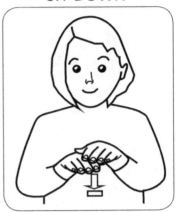

Palm down flat hands,
one on top of the other,
make short firm
movement down.

START, BEGIN

R. closed hand with
thumb up moves sharply
down behind L. flat hand.

START, BEGIN

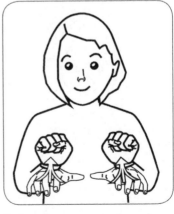

Palm down open hands
move sharply upwards as
they snap closed.

INSTRUCTIONS

DON'T, NOT, NO

Palm forward hand
sweeps firmly sideways as
head shakes. Both hands
can be used.

TALK, CHATTER

Fingers of bent hand
open and close onto
thumb several times.
Can be signed with two
hands.

LAUGH

'C' hands, one above the
other, make small side-to-
side shaking movements
under the chin.

SING

Palm back 'V' hands move
in upward circular
movements from near the
mouth. Can be signed
with just one hand.

INSTRUCTIONS

INSIDE, INDOORS

R. bent hand makes two short movements under L. hand.

OUTSIDE, OUTDOORS

Bent hand makes two short forward movements. One smooth forward arc gives another version for HOME.

CUT & PASTE

Index and middle fingers open and close several times (CUT) then R. flat hand flips over to palm down on L. palm (STICK).

DRAW

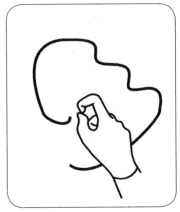

Hand moves in action of holding a pencil and drawing in the air.

PAINT

'N' hand sweeps up and down in brushing movements.

PICTURE, DIAGRAM

Index fingers move in outline shape of a sheet of paper. Can also mean CHART, LETTER.

KEYWORD

R. hand lands down onto tip of L. index (IMPORTANT) then palm forward narrow 'C' hand makes short forward movement (WORD).

WRITE, WRITE DOWN

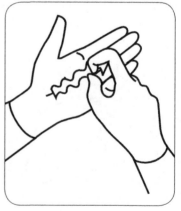

R. hand moves along L. palm with squiggling movements. Also means PEN, TAKE NOTES.

INSTRUCTIONS

DISCUSS

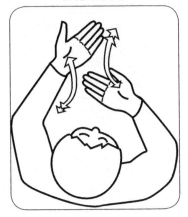

Palm up flat hands move backwards and forwards alternately several times. Also means CONVERSE.

PAIRS

Palm back 'V' hand shakes side-to-side several times.

INDIVIDUAL

Palm back R. index finger moves down and forward from behind L. palm back hand. Also means ALONE, INDEPENDENT.

SIT IN A CIRCLE

Open hands begin palm back and twist round/ back in a circle to finish palm forward.

INSTRUCTIONS

SHOW ME

Flat hand twists round to palm forward.

CHOOSE, PICK

Index finger closes onto thumb as hand moves backwards. May repeat, and with two hands alternately. Also means SELECT.

ROLE-PLAY

Palm forward 'O' hands move alternately backwards and forwards on chest several times. Also means PERFORM/ANCE.

TIME TO GO

R. index taps back of left wrist twice (TIME) then swings forward and away. (GO).

INSTRUCTIONS

COPY

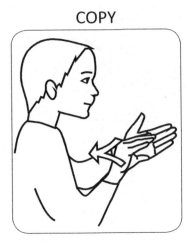

Thumb of R. bent hand closes onto fingers as hand moves backwards from L. palm.

DOWNLOAD

Thumb of R. bent hand closes onto fingers as it lands down onto L. palm and repeats several times.

NOT SURE, UNSURE

R. flat hand rests edge down on L. palm and waggles from side-to-side in wavering movements, lips are pressed together.

DON'T UNDERSTAND

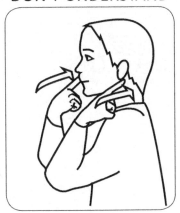

Index fingers flick backwards over the shoulders. Often with lip-pattern 'whoosh'. Also means OVER MY HEAD.

INSTRUCTIONS

THINK

Index finger taps or makes circular movements on side of forehead. May tap twice also meaning SENSIBLE.

REMEMBER, MEMORISE

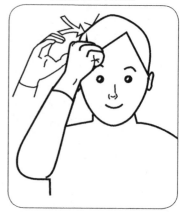

R. full 'C' hand closes to a fist at side of head.

FORGET, FORGOTTEN

Tips of bunched hand on forehead; hand springs open in forward movement.

CONCENTRATE, FOCUS

Flat hands at sides of the head move forward/down and curve in slightly.

INSTRUCTIONS

ASK

R. 'O' hand near side of mouth, moves forward in small arc.

ANSWER, REPLY, FEEDBACK

R. index near mouth flicks forward, as L. index held forward flicks back.

RIGHT, CORRECT

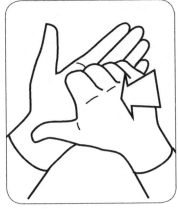

R. closed hand with thumb out bangs down onto L. palm.

WRONG

Edge of R. little finger bangs down on L. palm. May repeat. With raised eyebrows can mean 'WHAT'S WRONG?'

INSTRUCTIONS

CHECK

Index near eye and with little finger extended moves down changing to both 'Y' hands waggling alternately from the wrists.

LOOK

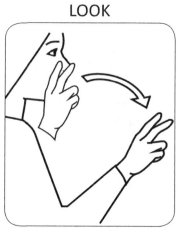

'V' hand makes short movement forward, or in direction to suit context.

LISTEN

Open hand moves to ear, closing to a bunched hand, or cupped hand held behind ear.

LEARN

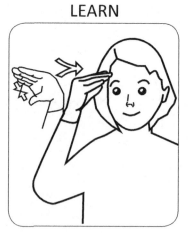

Palm forward hand closes sharply to a bunched hand as it twists back to side of head.

INSTRUCTIONS

READ

R. 'V' hand sweeps from side-to-side above L. palm.

SAY, TELL

Palm back index finger moves forward from the mouth.

INFORMATION, STORY

Palm back extended index fingers move quickly forwards and backwards alternately from the mouth.

EXPLAIN, STORY

Flat hands rotate round each other in forward circles eg *'I'll explain'* or backwards eg *'explain to me'*.

INSTRUCTIONS

NEXT, TURN

Extended thumb twists
over from palm down to
palm up in appropriate
direction.

SHARE

R. flat hand on L. palm
waggles from side to side
as hands move backwards
and forwards together.
Means SHARE USE OF.

YES

Closed hand nods up and
down as the head nods. Can
be head nod only to give a
positive response or confirm
a positive statement.

NO

Closed hand twists firmly from
the wrist with emphatic head
shake. Can be head shake only
for a negative response or to
emphasise a negative statement.

INSTRUCTIONS

STOP, FINISH, END

Fingers of bent hands close onto thumbs in short firm downward movement.

STAND UP, GET UP

Palm up flat hands move upwards.

PUT AWAY

Bunched hands move forward/down and open repeatedly in alternate movements.

TIDY UP

R. hand pats down onto the L. hand repeatedly as both hands move across to the right.

INSTRUCTIONS

LINE UP, QUEUE

Upright fingers are held in a line, one hand in front of the other, then pull apart.

QUICK, QUICKLY

R. index bounces quickly up and down off L. index with cheeks puffed for emphasis.

PLAY TIME

Palm up open hands move in small outward circles (PLAY) then R. index taps back of left wrist (TIME).

DINNER/LUNCH TIME

'N' hands move up and down to the mouth alternately (MEAL) then R. index taps back of left wrist (TIME).

INSTRUCTIONS

WAIT, NOT YET

Closed hands palm forward/down make repeated small inward circles.

WAIT, STOP, HOLD ON

Palm forward flat hands (or just one hand) make two short forward movements.

WASH HANDS

Hands rub together, twisting round each other. Also means SOAP.

HOME TIME

Tips of flat hands tap together, with hands held at an angle (HOME) then R. Index finger taps back of left wrist (TIME).

INSTRUCTIONS

TODAY, NOW

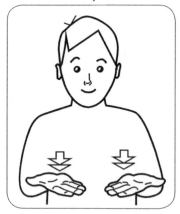

Palm up flat hands make two short movements down. Single firm movement for RIGHT NOW.

AFTER, LATER

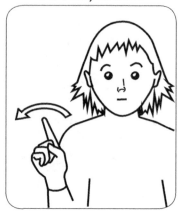

Palm forward index finger moves sideways in small arc. Movement may repeat.

TOMORROW

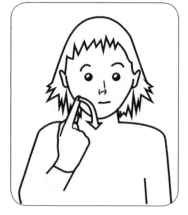

Index finger on side of cheek twists forward/down from the wrist to finish palm up. With 'V' hand means IN TWO DAYS.

YESTERDAY

Index finger on side of cheek twists back/down onto shoulder. With 'V' hand means TWO DAYS AGO.

INSTRUCTIONS

PRACTICE, TRAIN

R. palm down flat hand brushes forward twice against side of L. palm down flat hand.

IMPORTANT, CRUCIAL

R. open hand comes down to land on tip of L. index. May tap twice. Also means TOP.

WELL DONE

Closed hands with thumbs up make forward circles round each other towards person concerned. Also means CONGRATULATIONS.

BRILLIANT, FANTASTIC

R. closed hand with thumb up bangs on L. palm and bounces up again with lip-pattern 'vee'.

INSTRUCTIONS

LINK THE SIGN TO THE WORD

STORY

CHOOSE

LINE UP

ASK

READY

SHARE

NEXT

INFORMATION

Answers: 1 Next 2 Line up 3 Story 4 Ready 5 Ask 6 Share 7 Information 8 Choose.

108

A BIT ABOUT OTHER SIGN LANGUAGES

As stated in the introduction to this book, there are many different sign languages in existence all over the world.

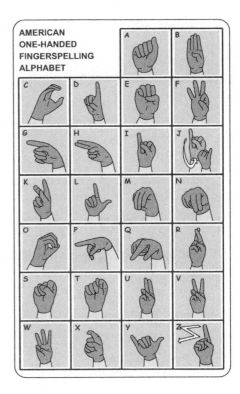

They are necessary to and highly valued by the Deaf communities through which they have evolved.

All are to some extent influenced by the spoken languages of their country but their integral visual spatial grammatical structures are very different to those used in spoken languages and each has its own vocabulary of signs.

There are many different fingerspelling alphabets too, most of them one-handed such as the American Sign Language (ASL) system above.

The sign languages of Australia (Auslan) and New Zealand (NZSL) are identifiably BSL based and use the two-handed alphabet but they have many unique signs in their vocabulary and also influences and borrowings from other sign languages such as ASL.

Like all languages, spoken and signed, BSL also has influences and borrowings from other languages - and like all living languages, it continues to evolve and develop.

USEFUL CONTACTS & RESOURCES

There are a number of specialist producers of teaching and learning materials in addition to the Let's Sign Series detailed on the back page.

Down Syndrome Training & Support Service Ltd

Registered charity run by & for parents
and carers of children who have Down Syndrome,
offering support and training.

2 Whitley Street, Bingley BD16 4JH
t: 01274 561308
e: office@downsyndromebradford.co.uk
w: www.downsupportbradford.btck.co.uk

LET'S SIGN BSL - Co-Sign Communications

(inc DeafBooks)
For the LET'S SIGN BSL teaching and learning resources.
e: info@letssign.co.uk
e: info@deafbooks.co.uk
w: www.LetsSign.co.uk
w: www.DeafBooks.co.uk

MeSign

British Sign Language Specialists.

The Office, The Robert Atkinson Centre,
Thornaby, Stockton-On-Tees TS17 8AP
t: 07792010630
e: hello@mesign.co.uk
w: www.mesign.co.uk

The National Deaf Children's Society   (NDCS)

National Office, Ground Floor South,
Castle House, 37- 45 Paul Street,
London EC2A 4LS
t: 020 7490 8656
e: ndcs@ndcs.org.uk
w: www.ndcs.org.uk

The School Sign Shop
Beautifully designed School Signage Boards including a range of BSL signs.

Unit 7 Moorswater Industrial Estate
Liskeard, Cornwall, PL14 4LN
t : 01579 340985
e: info@theschoolsignshop.co.uk
w: www.theschoolsignshop.co.uk

Royal Association for Deaf People (RAD)
RAD promote equality for Deaf people through the provision of accessible services.
t: 0845 688 2525 - **text phone:** 0845 688 2527
e: info@royaldeaf.org.uk
w: www.royaldeaf.org.uk

The Signing Company
Signs from British Sign Language (BSL) to teach signing to babies, children, families, educational practitioners and professionals.
e: enquiries@thesigningcompany.co.uk
w: www.thesigningcompany.co.uk

Widgit Software
Symbol Software & Let's Sign BSL graphics packs on licence.
1st Floor, Bishops House
Artemis Drive
Tachbrook Park
Warwick, CV34 6UD
t: 01926 333 680
e: info@widgit.com
w: www.widgit.com

USEFUL WEBSITES

www.abslta.org.uk
www.spreadthesign.com
www.rnid.org.uk
www.signbsl.com
www.bslzone.co.uk

www.signworldlearn.com
www.bslsignbank.ucl.ac.uk
www.bbc.co.uk/seehear
www.ssc.education.ed.ac.uk
www.signdictionary.co.uk

INDEX

Full alphabetical list of each sign and part sign so that new constructions can be made from the elements contained - e.g. HOME + WORK = HOMEWORK - PARENT + EVENING = PARENTS' EVENING and so on.

LET'S SIGN

British Sign Language (BSL) materials
for Early Years to Adult learners

Whole School Involvement

BSL & SSE Graphics Packs
(from Widgit.com/bsl)

Curriculum Support

Dictionaries, Books,
Guides, Kindles & Apps

NEW Mini TOPIC Books for
Learners
Early Years and Families

Posters,
Flashcards
& Stickers

See the full Let's Sign BSL Series
FREE DOWNLOADS

www.LetsSign.co.uk

for bulk order discounts, terms and enquiries
contact: info@letssign.co.uk - 01624 580505

Printed in Great Britain
by Amazon

86316356R00068